GETTYSBURG
AMAZING LITTLE KNOWN FACTS

by

HOWARD CALP

&

Copyright By ❧ Howard Calp
Published By ❧ Bob Wasel and MaryAnn Johnson-Bosler
Gettysburg, PA
2001

Acknowledgments

One person cannot write a book like this without the help of others. I would like to thank the friends and associates that took the time to help me with this publication. First of all I would like to thank several of my fellow Battlefield Guides for their input. I would like to say thank you to, Alan Crawford, Roy Frampton, James Hueting, Tim Smith, Don Walters, and the many other guides that have related stories in the Guide Room. For his expertise in proofreading this manuscript, a very special thanks to my friend and colleague, Jack Wise. I give a special thanks to Valerie Spindler for her artwork on the cover of this book and to Nancy Lauletta, Shirley Calp, and Susan Snyder for additional proofreading. Most important of all, a very special thanks to publishers, MaryAnn (Mimi) Johnson-Bosler and Bob Wasel, for the editing and pictures that appear in this book. Without their help, this book would not have been possible. Last, but not least, I would like to thank my wife, Shirley Calp, for her encouragement and patience with me to produce this publication.

Table of Contents

ಀ

Part I: National Cemetery

Almost immediately after the great battle, people knew the importance of what had occurred. We know that on November 19, 1863, the Soldiers' National Cemetery was dedicated by dignitaries. President Abraham Lincoln gave his now famous Gettysburg Address.

☙

There are over 3,500 Union soldiers interred in the cemetery that died at Gettysburg. It is known that Pennsylvania Governor Andrew Curtain, after arriving at the battlefield, was so appalled at what he saw that he directed Gettysburg attorney, David Wills, to act as his agent to establish a cemetery for the burial of the Union dead.

☙

A 17-acre plot of ground that is now the Soldiers' National Cemetery was purchased at a cost of $2,475.87. It cost $1.59 per body to bury the Union soldiers there. Samuel Weaver was given the position as Superintendent of Exhumations.

☙

There are approximately 3,512 bodies of Civil War soldiers interred there, 979 are completely unknown and 1,664 are partially unknown. Not generally acknowledged and often asked about is the Confederate dead. That is the saddest aspect of all concerning the aftermath of the battle.

☙

The South was so devastated after the Civil War that it did not have the funds for the burial of its soldiers. The North did not want the Confederates buried in the same ground that was consecrated for the Union. The Confederate men lay in makeshift graves on the battlefield and remained there until 1872. At that time the Southern Ladies' Memorial Association was established and funds became available for the removal and reburial of the dead. The post-war re-interments occurred in Richmond, Charleston, Savannah, and Raleigh. Approximately 3,320 bodies were transferred to cemeteries in these cities. The cost per body was $3.25.

In the Soldiers' National Cemetery, the bronze statue of Union General John F. Reynolds was cast out of Confederate cannon barrels. This was a tribute to him from the surviving members of the First Corp of the Army of the Potomac, which he had commanded.

ℰℴ

The first unofficial monument on the Gettysburg battlefield was the Minnesota Urn erected in the Minnesota plot of the cemetery in 1867. To honor their fellow soldiers who died during the battle the surviving members of the First Minnesota regiment funded this urn.

ℰℴ

In the Soldiers' National Cemetery, there are metal plaques that contain parts of a poem titled, "The Bivouac of the Dead."

After the Mexican War, Theordore O' Hara wrote this poem:

The Bivouac of the Dead

The muffled drum sad roll has beat
The soldiers' last tattoo
No more on life's parade shall meet
That brave and fallen few.
On fame's eternal camping ground
Their silent tents are spread
And glory guards with solemn round.
The bivouac of the dead.
Rest on embalmed and sainted dead!
Dear as the blood ye gave;
No impious footstep here shall tread
The herbage of your grave;
Nor shall your glory be forgot
While fame her record keeps.
Or honor points the hallowed spot
Where valor proudly sleeps.

President Lincoln was 54 years old when he delivered the Gettysburg Address on November 19, 1863. The 12 ft. x 20 ft. wooden platform on which he delivered his immortal Gettysburg Address was actually in Evergreen Cemetery, not the Soldiers' National Cemetery.

&

In Evergreen Cemetery there is a tombstone that was struck by an artillery projectile during the battle. The grave is that of Sgt. Fredrick Huber of the 23rd Pa. Infantry, killed at the battle of Fair Oaks, Va., May 31, 1862.

There are five copies of the Gettysburg Address: 1) Nicolay copy – located in the Library of Congress; 2) Hay copy – located in the Library of Congress; 3) Everett copy – located in the Illinois Historical Library; 4) Bancroft copy – located at Cornell University; 5) Bliss copy – located in the Lincoln Room of the White House, purchased for $54,000 in 1949.

It has been said that Lincoln wrote the Gettysburg Address on a torn piece of paper or a discarded envelope he found while on the train to Gettysburg. This is a myth. It is known that Lincoln's speech was, in fact, written on White House stationary and was almost completed in the White House before he came to Gettysburg. Lincoln finished it while he stayed at the home of David Wills in Gettysburg. When Lincoln came to Gettysburg in November of 1863, he was suffering from smallpox and was very ill. When he returned to Washington after the ceremony, he was sick in bed for several days.

The iron fence that today divides the Soldiers' National Cemetery from the civilian Evergreen Cemetery was in fact the same fence that surrounded Lafayette Park in Washington, D. C.

$$\Omega$$

Part II: Monuments

The first official monument on the battlefield is the monument to the 2nd Massachusetts, near Culp's Hill, dedicated in 1879. One of the newest monuments on the battlefield is the Delaware Memorial, dedicated April 29, 2000.

☙

At the 75th reunion, nearly 1,800 Civil War veterans attended. Their average age at that time was 94. At this reunion, President Franklin D. Roosevelt officially dedicated the Eternal Light Peace Memorial. The base of the memorial is made of Maine granite. The shaft is made of Alabama limestone, which symbolizes north and south united once again.

☙

In March of 1963, President John F. Kennedy and his wife were touring the battlefield as many visitors do today. Of the over 1,300 monuments and markers on the battlefield, the Kennedys were captivated by the Eternal Light Peace Memorial. Many people believe that after President Kennedy was assassinated and buried in Arlington National Cemetery, the eternal flame on his grave may have been from the remembrance of the flame on this monument. There is really no documented proof of this, but it is an interesting concept.

On McPherson's Ridge, at the base of the John Buford statue are four cannons. These cannons represent Battery "A" 2nd U.S. Artillery. The cannon barrel that is pointing toward the stone building, which is today the west end guide station, is cannon #233. This cannon barrel has been documented as the one that fired the very first Union cannon shot of the battle of Gettysburg.

The Pennsylvania Memorial was dedicated in 1910 at an unheard of cost at that time of $182,000. It is the largest memorial on the battlefield today. At the base of the memorial are bronze tablets listing the names of approximately 34,000 Union soldiers from the state of Pennsylvania that fought at the battle of Gettysburg. The image on the top of the memorial is Nike, the goddess of victory and peace.

ဢ

The Virginia Memorial is one of the most impressive on the entire battlefield. F. William Sievers sculpted this memorial in 1917 at a cost of $50,000. It is made of bronze and granite. The image at the top has been considered the very best likeness of Robert E. Lee ever cast in bronze as stated by people that actually knew the General.

Gettysburg National Military Park is the only battlefield that has a monument to Confederate General James Longstreet.

෴

In the area of Culp's Hill, there are four monuments for soldiers from the State of Maryland. One is Confederate, the 2nd Maryland (C.S.A.). Three are Union, Potomac Home Brigade, 1st Eastern Shore, and 3rd Maryland (U.S.A.). Marylander fought Marylander on Culp's Hill. The state of Maryland never formally seceded from the Union, but supplied troops to both armies.

෴

The Alabama Memorial, located on South Confederate Avenue, was dedicated in 1933. Take notice of the figure of the Confederate soldier to the right. Does the face look familiar to you? It should. This is the image of the Father of our Country, George Washington.

Ω

Part III: Weapons and Ammunition

Approximately fifty percent of the Confederate artillery ammunition turned out to be unfunctionable due to poor manufacturing in the south.

The Confederates had two British Whitworth cannons at Gettysburg during the battle. They had the effective range of three miles. These cannons were the only breech-loading cannons at Gettysburg. Breech-loading means they were loaded from the rear of the barrel. The other cannons were loaded from the front of the barrel and are called muzzle-loaders.

One of the most popular muzzle-loading cannons was the Napoleon used by both armies. This cannon, named after Napoleon III of France, fired a 12-pound solid cannonball at a maximum range of 1,680 yards.

Ω

The 10-pound rifled Parrott cannon was popular in both armies. This weapon fired a 10-pound explosive projectile with an effective range of one-and-one-half miles. You can always recognize these cannons when you see them because they have the iron band in the rear of the barrel for reinforcement.

Ω

It is reported that the Confederate artillery at Gettysburg contained such a mixture of different cannons that it became difficult to supply them with the correct ammunition. The Union army had more uniformity in their cannons thus they could be better supplied.

Ω

The civil war bullets, called minie balls, that soldiers on both sides used, were similar. Depending on the manufacturer, the difference between the Union minie ball and the Confederate minie ball was that the Union minie ball had three rings, where as the Confederate had two. The model "61" Springfield rifled musket had an effective range of 3 to 5 hundred yards.

Part IV: The Battlefield and Town

Years after the Civil War, there were three large reunions of Civil War veterans at Gettysburg. The first reunion was the 25th Anniversary of the battle held in 1888. The second was the 50th Anniversary in 1913. The last was held in 1938, the 75th Anniversary of the battle.

ဆ

At the time of the battle, the town of Gettysburg was smaller than it is today. According to the 1860 census, the town consisted of roughly 2,400 people. There were about 450 buildings that made up the town. Today approximately 188 of these buildings still stand, and many show battle damage.

ဆ

Founded in 1826, the Lutheran Theological Seminary is considered the oldest functioning Lutheran Seminary in the entire nation.

ဆ

Spangler's Spring, at the base of Culp's Hill, has been a source of controversy for many years. It was reported that Union and Confederate soldiers drank water from this spring at the same time. This was not the case. Although both sides did in fact drink the water from this spring, it was at a time when the respective side occupied the area.

ဆ

The house today referred to as Lee's headquarters, was at the time the residence of a widow by the name of Mary Thompson. It was actually owned by Congressman Thaddeus Stevens.

After the battle, there were approximately 113 makeshift field hospitals in town. Practically any building that was standing during or after the battle served in one way or another as a field hospital. Camp Letterman was established about a mile east of town to care for the wounded of both armies. It served as the main field hospital in Gettysburg until it ceased operation in November of 1863 when the last of the patients were transferred to Philadelphia and Baltimore.

℣

On the southern end of the battlefield, there is a large out-cropping of boulders called Devil's Den; no one really knows how it got this name. One popular story is that many years before the Civil War, this out-cropping of boulders was infested with rattlesnakes. Local farmers in the area would let their livestock graze in the valley near the rocks. The snakes would bite the livestock if they wandered too close to the den. The farmers got together, and, with torch in hand, attempted to rid the den of the poisonous reptiles. It seems that they were successful except for one crafty old rattler. The farmers said, "He is as crafty as the devil." No matter how hard they tried, they could not get rid of this snake. To this day, the area of the boulders is known as Devil's Den.

The original battlefield encompassed approximately 25 square miles. Today the battlefield that is being maintained by the federal government is approximately 6,000 acres. There are approximately 32 miles of roadway running in and about the park. There are 32

restored historical farms.

Ω

Part V: Leaders, Soldiers, and Civilians

Many Presidents have visited Gettysburg throughout the years. One President actually settled here, the 34th President of the United States, Dwight D. Eisenhower. In World War I, Major Dwight D. Eisenhower was in charge of an army training facility at Gettysburg called Camp Colt. After his second term as President he and his wife moved to Gettysburg. He purchased a farm in the area during his administration and raised beef cattle that he was very proud of. Many dignitaries visited the Eisenhowers during their years at Gettysburg, including Charles De Gaulle and British Field Marshall Bernard Law Montgomery. President Eisenhower lived on the farm until his death in 1969. His wife, Mamie, resided there until her death in 1979, when the property was given to the federal government and is now the Eisenhower Historic Site.

୫

At the time of the battle 47 year old Union General George Gordon Meade was the commander of the Union army at Gettysburg. He was a graduate of West Point Military Academy, class of 1835 and 19th in his class. Meade's parents were in Cadiz, Spain on a business trip where on December 31, 1815 George Gordon Meade was born.

୫

Robert E. Lee, commander of the Confederate army at Gettysburg, was 56 years old. Lee had also graduated from West Point Military Academy, class of 1829 and was 2nd in his class.

15

The man who graduated first in Robert E. Lee's class was a man by the name of Charles Mason, who never pursued a military career. Mason became a chief executive for the railroads that would eventually aid the Union war effort.

&

During the battle of Gettysburg, it is believed that Confederate General Robert E. Lee had what was known at that time as the soldier's trot. It was also known as dysentery and today is known as diarrhea.

Lee had five horses during the Civil War: Traveller, Lucy Long, Roan, Richmond, and Ajax. At the battle of Gettysburg, it is known that Traveller and Lucy Long were with him. His favorite was Traveller who was in Lee's funeral procession in Lexington, Virginia in 1870.

&

A.L. Long, Robert E. Lee's personal aide, reports that Lee had a pet chicken named "Hen." Lee was very fond of this chicken, and, it appears, that the chicken was very fond of Lee. Long reports that this chicken was kept at Lee's headquarters' tent. Every morning the chicken would lay an egg under Lee's cot. Lee would have this egg for breakfast. Fortunately, Hen did survive the battle of Gettysburg, but did not survive the Civil War. It is believed that Hen became a meal herself.

During the three days of battle in Gettysburg, only one civilian fatality occurred. On July 3rd, Mary Virginia Wade, also known as Jennie Wade, was in the home of her sister baking bread for the Union soldiers. As the story goes, a stray bullet pierced two doors striking her in the back, killing her instantly. Her body was taken to the basement of the house by relatives and kept there until the battle was over. She was then buried in the back yard. Her body was later disinterred and buried in a church cemetery in town. A few years after that she was again reburied, this time in Evergreen Cemetery, where she rests to this day. By an act of Congress, the American flag may fly over her grave twenty-four hours a day without being illuminated at night.

℘

The story of Wesley Culp is unique in itself. Wesley was born and raised in Gettysburg, and was a carriage maker by trade. Prior to the Civil War, Wesley moved to what was then Sheppardstown, Virginia, now West Virginia. When the war broke out, Wesley joined the 2nd Virginia infantry of the famous Stonewall Brigade. During the fighting on Culp's Hill, Wesley was killed on the property belonging to his family. His body was never found. It is believed, however, that his Gettysburg relatives secretly found and buried him in an unknown location. His relatives were concerned that, since Wesley fought for the Confederacy, people of the town would desecrate his grave.

℘

Another interesting character was John Burns. Burns was a civilian who fought with the Union soldiers on McPherson's Ridge during the first day's battle. Burns was wounded and became a sort of a folk hero after the battle. It seems that Burns liked to exaggerate about certain aspects of his life. He told people that he was wounded four, five, and even six times during the fighting on July 1st. Burns also stated that he was a veteran of the War of 1812 and fought at Lundy's Lane. Recent research has revealed that Burns was indeed a

17

veteran of the War of 1812, but did not fight at Lundy's Lane. Burns was stationed in a camp near Philadelphia, but never saw battle action during that war.

෧

Union Major General John F. Reynolds was the highest-ranking officer killed at Gettysburg. Reynolds was killed fifteen minutes after arriving on the battlefield. His body was eventually buried in Lancaster, Pennsylvania, his hometown. Lancaster is about fifty miles east of Gettysburg.

෧

Union General Daniel Sickles is another intriguing person. Prior to the Civil War, he shot and killed the son of Francis Scott Key in Lafayette Park in Washington, D. C. Sickles shot Key for having an affair with his wife. Sickles was arrested, tried for murder, and was the first person in this country to successfully use the defense of "Not guilty by reason of temporary insanity." Believe it or not, he was acquitted of the charges.

During the bloody fighting of July 2nd on the southern end of the battlefield, General Sickles was severely wounded after being struck in the right leg by a cannon ball. Sickles was taken a short distance to a temporary field hospital where what was left of the leg was amputated. He had the leg preserved and sent to Washington, D. C. to the Museum of Medicine and Pathology. The leg bone, stripped of flesh, is still housed there today. Sickles would take people to the museum after the war and show them his severed limb.

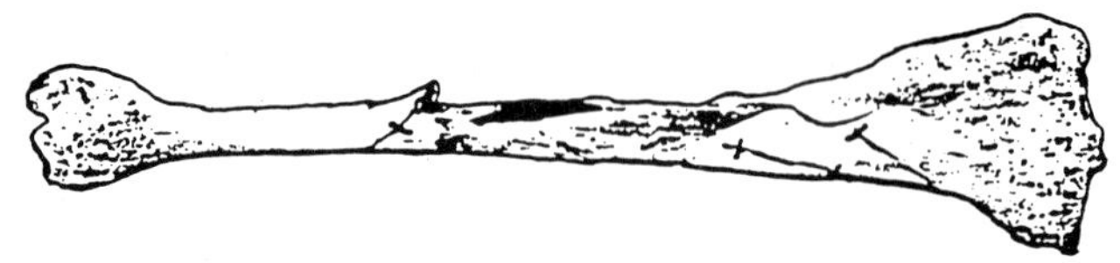

The battlefield location where Sickles was wounded is located to the left of the Trostle barn. A monument displaying a diamond on its top marks the spot. Looking at the barn, you can see where a cannon shell was fired through it.

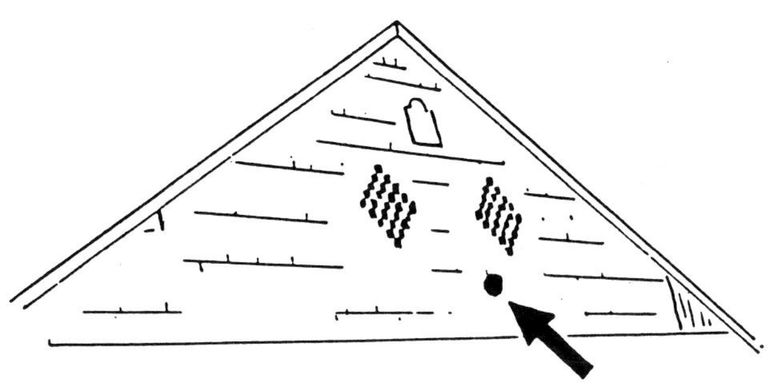

Sickles became the last surviving Corp commander at Gettysburg. He died fifty-one years after losing his leg on the field of battle.

૭

After the Civil War, Joshua L. Chamberlain of the famous 20th Maine regiment served as governor of Maine for four terms. Chamberlain's horse was named Charlemagne.

૭

Union General Winfield Scott Hancock was severely wounded on the afternoon of July 3rd. While his men were battling Pickett's infantry, a bullet struck his saddle driving a saddle nail approximately six inches into his groin, almost causing him to bleed to death.

Union General George Meade's horse was named Old Baldy. The horse was wounded nine times during the Civil War. After Old Baldy died, his head was mounted on the wall at the Grand Army of the Republic museum in Philadelphia. It is still there today.

⁗

After the battle of Gettysburg, members of George Armstrong Custer's Michigan brigade began to wear navy jumpers, just as their flamboyant leader had been wearing. They also started wearing red scarves around their necks.

⁗

There were sixty-two Congressional Medal of Honor recipients in the battle of Gettysburg.

⁗

At the Battle of Gettysburg there were troops from Florida numbering approximately seven hundred soldiers. After the fighting on July 2nd and 3rd, there were close to 445 casualties. A man in one of the Florida regiments became infamous after the Civil War. This man's name was Lewis Powell, a.k.a. "Lewis Paine," one of the conspirators in the Lincoln assassination. Powell stabbed Secretary Seward with a large knife at the same time that John Wilkes Booth was assassinating the President. Powell was tried, convicted in the plot, and hanged at the old Capitol Prison in Washington, D. C. along with co-conspirators Mary Surratt, George Atzerodt, and David Herold.

⁗

Colonel Cross was killed on the afternoon of July 2nd while leading his troops on the southern end of the battlefield. It is believed that on that day he may have had a premonition of his own

20

death. Cross had a habit of wearing a red bandanna around his head when he went into battle. On July 2nd, he was seen wearing a black bandanna. As he was marching into battle General Hancock shouted to him, "Colonel, by the end of this day you will be wearing a star." This meant that he would be promoted to the rank of General. Cross replied, "No sir, for I fear that this is my last battle." Cross, of course, was right. Today, the 5th New Hampshire monument marks the spot where Cross fell.

General Pickett came to Gettysburg with only three of his five brigades; Armistead, Kemper, and Garnett. Corse and Jenkin's brigades remained in Virginia to help protect the Confederate Capitol of Richmond.

Pickett held Lee responsible for the failure of the attack for the rest of his life. After the war, Pickett, as well as former Confederate Colonel John Mosby, visited Lee. After the meeting it is reported that Pickett turned to Mosby and said, "That man cost me my division at Gettysburg." Mosby turned back to Pickett and stated, "Yes, George, but he made your name immortal."

&

It is reported that, at the battle of Gettysburg, Confederate

General A. P. Hill was suffering from a venereal disease that he had contracted at West Point Military Academy during his time there as a cadet. This was the reason that he played such a minor role in the battle.

૨૭

Confederate General Richard Ewell had been wounded about a year before the battle of Gettysburg. His leg had been amputated, and, while at Gettysburg, the stump of the leg became inflamed. He soaked the stump in Rock Creek to relieve the pain. Ewell rode in a horse and buggy, as this was the easiest way for him to travel.

૨૭

An interesting aspect of the battle seemed to be the absence of Confederate General Jeb Stuart and his Confederate cavalry during the battle of Gettysburg. In Robert E. Lee's orders to Stuart on June 22, 1863, Lee ordered Stuart to stay south of the Potomac River until he was sure that the Union army had crossed over to the northern side. Lee then directed Stuart to proceed across the river and destroy all railroad and communication lines, and then obtain as many supplies as he could handle. After that, he was to proceed to the right of General Ewell. Lee also directed Stuart to leave approximately 2,500 cavalrymen in an area controlled by General Longstreet. Lee repeated this order to Stuart again on June 23, 1863.

When people condemn Stuart for not being at Gettysburg to provide proper scouting for the Confederate army, they should consider Lee's order itself. When Stuart left the 2,500 cavalrymen, why didn't Longstreet use them for the necessary scouting? Longstreet had these men guarding the mountain passes in the rear of the Confederate army. Although this was very important, Longstreet did not need all of them for that purpose. A small portion could have been used to provide information as to the whereabouts of the Union army.

In addition, Stuart had captured a Union wagon train of nearly 125 supply-laden wagons in Rockville, Maryland. Usually wagons travel at a speed of two to three miles per hour, which would have slowed up Stuart's movements. At the time Lee issued the orders to Stuart, neither was aware that there would be a battle at Gettysburg. Had Jeb Stuart acted differently, he would then have disobeyed Lee's orders. This information is located in the Official Records of the Civil War.

⅋

There is a myth that the Confederates came to Gettysburg on July 1st for shoes. In the first place, there was never a shoe factory in Gettysburg. Prior to the fighting, Lee issued orders to his officers not to bring on any general engagement with the enemy until the entire Confederate army was up and concentrated. Confederate General Henry Heth engaged the enemy on the morning of July 1st, and before long, a general engagement ensued. Heth wrote in his official report that he heard that there was a stash of shoes in the town of Gettysburg, and he decided to get them even though it meant disobeying Lee's orders.

Heth never explained where he had heard about the shoes. What was known at the time was that part of General Ewell's Corp had passed through Gettysburg on June 26th. They had demanded, with threats of destroying the town if their demands were not met, certain supplies, as well as money, from the town officials. They not only got shoes, they also acquired food and many other supplies. Most of their demands were met.

It is believed that General Heth wrote this in his report to clear his name. He disobeyed Lee's orders and he knew it. It is believed that he meant to capture some militia troops for General Lee on the morning of July 1st as a prize. He did not know that what he was actually dealing with were seasoned veteran cavalrymen and not local militia as he first thought.

Part VI: The Battle and Aftermath

The battle of Culp's Hill, on the morning of July 3rd,
was the only time during the battle that the Union army
would go on a major offensive against the Confederate army. It is
reported that after the fighting on Culp's Hill, Confederate bodies
were stacked up like cordwood.

ꝏ

The weather during the battle, as recorded by Professor
Jacobs at Pennsylvania College, was as follows: July 1st, 2:00 P. M.,
76° July 2nd, 81°; and July 3rd, 87°.

ꝏ

After the famous Pickett's Charge failed, a sixteen foot plank
was removed from the fence that bordered the Emmittsburg Road. It
was discovered that the board contained approximately eight hundred
bullet holes.

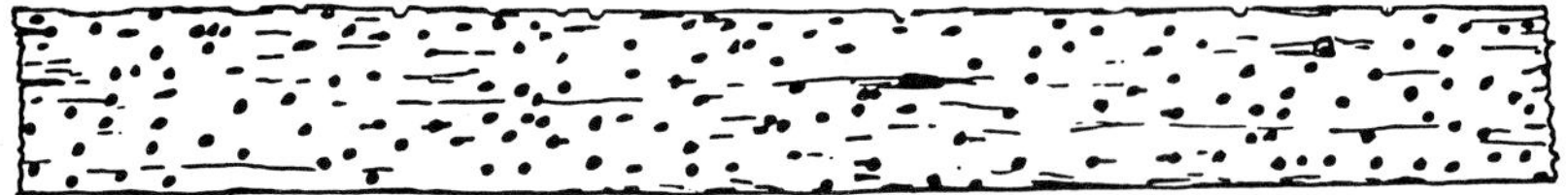

At the start of Pickett's charge, the artillery bombardment lasted approximately two hours. The actual infantry attack itself endured only fifty minutes. Of the 12,000 Confederate soldiers that initiated the attack, about half would be casualties.

ജ

It is reported that, as Lee was removing his troops from the battlefield on July 4th, the wagon train of Confederate wounded stretched nearly seventeen miles in length.

ജ

It is believed that the Union wagons, limbers, caissons, and ambulances, forming a line, would reach from Gettysburg to the Inner Harbor in Baltimore, Maryland —a distance of about 52 miles.

ജ

The famous Wheatfield was the scene of bloody carnage on the afternoon of July 2nd. The field changed hands approximately six times within two hours and when the fighting was over, it contained about 6,000 casualties. The wheat was about waist high on an average man, but in two hours it was trampled completely flat and bloodstained. Eyewitness accounts stated that you could walk across the 23-acre plot of ground by just stepping on the dead bodies, never touching the ground.

As Lee was removing his army from Gettysburg on July 4th, Vicksburg, Mississippi had fallen to the forces under U. S. Grant.

એ

When the armies came to Gettysburg they brought with them over 90,000 horses and mules. By the end of the battle roughly 5,000 of them lay dead on the battlefield. Later, the dead horses were dragged to areas of the field where they were burned. It is reported that it took about a week to burn one average pile of dead horses.

After the battle of Gettysburg, Lee had lost about one third of his army. Meade had lost nearly three of his seven-infantry corps. Lee was not able to replace his soldiers since the South's manpower had dwindled due to previous wartime losses. The Union army, however, had what seemed to be an unlimited resource of men and supplies. This is the reason that Lee was forced to surrender his army at Appomattox, Virginia to U. S. Grant on April 9th, 1865.

These amazing little known facts are some of the interesting parts of the battle of Gettysburg --- and there are many, many more.